WHAT WAS I THINKING?

Featuring: "The Night I Killed Nichaleous", "Green is not my Color", "The Tribal Dance Of The Hairy Neck Mud Stomper" and many other often requested favorites.

GREG BULLOCK

What was I Thinking?

Copyright © 2020 by Gregory A Bullock.

This book is a work of fiction based on the Aurthors past expériences. Names, characters, businesses, organizations, places, events and incidents either are the product of the author's imagination or are used fictitiously. Any resemblance to actual persons, living or dead, events, or locales is entirely coincidental.

For information contact : Greg Bullock

1gabullock@gmail.com

Book and Cover design by G.A.Bullock

First Edition: March 2020

42653

Table of Contents

Chapter One

A ROSE BY ANY OTHER NAME WOULD SMELL....

The young surgeon's hands trembled as he started to make the final incision. Fear immobilized him with the realization that the patient was now awake and feeling the pain from the procedure. Head spinning he dropped the scalpel and ran for the nearest doorway. Leaving his assistant to deal with the situation. and dropping to his knees as nausea overtook him he noticed that his assistant was already outside and looking pale. The patient had been left alone to fend for herself..........

Sitting on a deer stand last year I was amazed to see a large black and white animal crossing the open field that I was hunting. For a while I could not tell what it was. Unusually large this skunk was different from the ones that I had seen in my youth. Instead of having the white stripes running down the center of it's back, the animal had long hair that touched the ground all the way around it. As it walked along the hair flowing gave the appearance that the animal was floating. The white stripes were not on it's back but down low on the long hair much like fringe on a garment. It was beautiful. As it passed below me I could not help wanting to take it home. Then I remembered a hunt that I had gone on years ago when I was just a teenager.

That particular evening I had been squirrel hunting in the woods behind our home when I grew tired. Sitting on the ground next to a tree resting I soon heard footsteps approaching from behind. Thinking it must be a deer, I set perfectly still until it seemed that the creature could not have been more than three feet behind the tree where I was. In one smooth motion I lifted my gun and rolled to the side on my stomach prepared to shoot . Only then did I realize that I had misjudged the distance the noise was from me and was face to face with a polecat who was as startled as I was.

If the judges would only have been there I am sure that I would have scored at least a nine point four on a scale of ten for the gymnastic routine that I performed. I had it all down, style, height, number of revolutions, speed and most importantly distance. Gathering my composure I moved quickly to a new area to hunt not wanting to intrude or inconvenience *PePe La Pue'* any further.

Soon caught up in the excitement of a new hunt. I found myself waiting for a squirrel to reveal himself for a clean shot when suddenly I felt something rub against my leg. Afraid it was a snake I looked down toward the ground only to see that it was the same skunk. Funny how it looked smaller from way up here in the tree. (I'm sure that the judges would have given me a nine point eight for this one). James wrote, *"to flee the very appearance of evil"*, I want you to know by now I'm thinking that this skunk must be pretty evil. So I obeyed the word of God and fled.

Romance is a hard thing to understand. Who can explain why people fall in love. Everyone's taste is different. I'll admit that at first I was as shocked as anyone would be. But as I said who can explain. You guessed it, my furry friend had fallen in love. For you see everywhere that I went she arrived not far behind me. Finally I gave up trying to hunt, made the decision to never wear skunk scent in the woods again, and headed home.

Early the next morning I went into town with my parents and was gone for several hours. Upon arriving home I found my best friend sitting on our doorsteps with a paper bag and a hard-bound book on the step beside him. Pulling me aside he said, "Just wait until you see what I have in the bag". Jerking open the bag to look inside my reflexes took over as I threw the bag up in the air and began to run in place, there was the same skunk that I had run from the day before.

"What did you do that for," my friend ask. After explaining my reaction, my friend told me that he intended to make a pet out of it. "I was in the garden this morning," he said. "When this ole skunk walked right up to me and started rubbing against my leg. Just like a house cat. So I'm gonna deskunk it." "You don't know anything about doing that I said." "Sure I do," he continued. "I went to the library this morning and got this book on how to do it. Nothing to it, it's a snap and you are going to help me, because it takes two people to do it ya know."

After much discussion I caved to the pressure and agreed to help. The book said that we need to take either and put the animal to sleep. Fourteen year old boys don't have a lot of either laying around so we used what we could find in my dad's work shop. "Yes sir", my friend said with authority. "This will do it for sure, if you can't find either good old WD_40 and starter fuel will do it every time."

Opening the top of the paper bag a crack we emptied the contents of the two cans into the bag and folded the top down for a few minutes. My friend was right, it made that skunk sleep real good. As my friend held the skunk with it's tail bent back over it's back I started the operation, just like the book said. There are two glands to remove, gland number one was successful. I was proud. Surgery on gland number two began.

Six inches from my face, gland two held with tweezers, razor blade in my right hand, beginning the incision, the skunk woke up.

"*When sin is finished it brings forth death.*" You know a skunk is still just a skunk. You can bath and brush it. You can pet and feed it. You can teach it to do tricks. You can put it on a leash. You can even give it a name, but it is still just a skunk.

Sin is like that, we can bring it home with us, remove part of it , dress it up, try to tame it, get others to accept it, even rename it. But it is still sin, and we need to realize that. It's time that we go back to calling it by it's real name. It's time that we remember that it stinks, and it's ugly and that end the end it always either steals, kills or destroys. It is not enough that we just don't partake in sin. We need to see it for what it really is and to be repulsed at even the thought of it. I want my eyes to see through all the glitter and glitz and recognize all the hideous evil that is hidden below the surface. Sitting up in my deer stand I was so thankful that I was not in any danger. This new type of skunk never looked up he never knew that I was there. May we all find a place to hide in the Lords Pavilion where we are so surrounded by the presence of God that sin can no longer locate where are. An may we be smart enough not to climb down and try to pet it.

Chapter Two

BEFORE THE ROOSTER CROWS
"Help me, Help me, somebody please help!"

My brother killed the ignition switch of his pickup truck. As the radio became silent he opened the door and listened. The morning was still; a brilliant sunrise painted the surface of the lake with an orange and yellow hue. For a few moments he waited alone hearing nothing except the sound of the water as the waves crashed into the shoreline. "I must be hearing things, he thought to himself as he gathered his fishing rod and can of bait and headed for the water's edge. As he baited his hook and was making his first cast he heard the cry again. "Help me, help, somebody please help!" As he dropped his fishing rod he scanned the surface of the lake for someone in trouble. But saw nothing. "Help, help!" This time he located the sound, it wasn't coming from the water at all. It was coming from the direction of a nearby cabin.

Rushing to the cabin he found that the doors were locked. As he circled around he called out, "Don't worry, help is on the way. Just tell me where you are."

"Help me, please help me. I'm under here," came the cry. Dropping to his knees he looked under the cabin.

The lake house was an old building, built from rough cut pine siding. The main house was sitting about three feet off of the ground on piers made from saw cut sections of a cypress log. The exterior of the building was surrounded by dense underbrush. The under the side of the building was floored with a layer soft bare mud. Scattered about were small pools of water. Running lengthwise across the center of the entire building was a section of hogwire fence. Evidently placed there ages ago with the intent of keeping the dogs contained in the back yard, yet providing them with some shelter from times of harsh weather.

As his vision became adjusted to the dim light beneath the cabin Kirk could not believe his eyes. Lying prostate before him on the ground was the long skinny figure of a man. The man was completely coated in mud from the top of his head to the bottom of his bare feet. Clutched tightly in his right hand was whisky bottle whose contents were almost expired. From the glazed look on the man's face Kirk could tell that he was fairly well drunk. "Help me, I cant let it go!" he spoke.

"Are you hurt?" Kirk asks.

"No I just can't let go."

"Let go of what?"

"Come around to the other side of the house and go under and hold it until I get out," he cried. "Hurry".

Bewildered Kirk crawled out from under the house and ran around to the opposite side of the cabin. As he crawled under this time he was facing the distressed man. Pausing he surveyed the situation. There in front of him, now on the opposite side of the hogwire fence was Dudly Badd. The town drunk of the small community several miles back down the road. His left arm was pushed through the webbing of the fence and in his hand he was tightly clutching the leg of an oversize Rhode Island Red Rooster who looked to be in no better shape than his captor. As the ridiculousness of the situation began to become apparent it was hard to define just who was the captor and who was the captive. Unless Dudley loosened his grip on the rooster he could not withdraw his hand, so in many ways he was no better off than the bird he held.

The morning before, Dudley had awakened with a tremendous hangover, holding his throbbing head he realized that it was the crowing of the rooster that had awakened him. "I am going to kill that rooster," Dudley thought. "Yea, I am going to kill him and have him for lunch. I'll put a stop to his crowing." With that Dudley grabbed a new bottle of spirits staggered outside and the pursuit began. That was yesterday morning and now a full day later help was finally on the way. The details of the chase are still sketchy, but the end result was that Dudley was under the house holding a Rooster by the leg through the fence. And was too drunk to realize that all he had to do was let it go.

There have been roosters in my life that I too have hated. When I was three or four my grandmother had a big red rooster that would chase me around the barnyard, pecking at me as I ran as fast as I could. Then when I was a teenager slipping in the house late a night (after my curfew) when my parents were asleep. We had on old rooster that would get out of bed, jump up on the fence right outside of my dad's window and crow his heart out. Not just once but seemingly every time that I was late. Naturally this would awaken my dad who would then come and spend some time bonding with me.

Those two were just plain aggravating but there is a rooster that I have hated even more than any rooster that I have ever personally encountered. Every time I hear the story cold chills run down my spine. It is as if it is my story that is being told, instead of the story of that great man of God. Only moments after he had sworn his allegiance. Jesus turned to Peter and said, "Verily I say unto thee, That this night, before the cock crow, thou shall deny me thrice. Then later, in Matthew 24:74 Peter said, *".... I do not know the man."* The Bible says, *"And the cock crew."*

The rooster crowed, when I first read it I cried. To me the crowing of the rooster signified the end, a closure to a chapter. The door shutting to a wonderful experience. Leaving the man empty, the past few years of his life wasted in pursuit of something that he now would never have. I soon expected to find him a broken derelict, or possibly hanging from the same tree with Judas or some other similar fate. Then Easter came and went.

We can never change what they did to Jesus, the beatings, the ridicule, the humiliation, the crucifixion, then the murder. We can't even change the things that we ourselves did yesterday.

The tomb is empty. Jesus does live. And Grace does abound both now as well as then. When the angel appeared to Mary at the tomb, he told her *to "Go your way, go tell the disciples and Peter, that He goeth before you into Galilee: there you shall see him…".* Jesus wanted Peter to be sure and know that he was forgiven, and that Jesus still loved him. The crowing of the rooster wasn't the signal of the ending instead it was a trumpet of a new beginning. Our Lord wanted us to be sure and know that we could come back to him at any point in our fleshly walk here on earth. Jesus did come to seek and to save we who were lost. We can return to him any time that we decide to let go of the things that are keeping us away. The choice is ours.

Every time we compromise our walk, every time we walk in opposition to his word we are in a sense denying him. We often find

One day Peter said, "I go a fishing" and he did. The Christ had been crucified and Peter had denied him. The ministry he had planned had crumbled and with no direction for his future he returned to the trade that he

 knew… fishing. After a long night of wasted effort, the Master called to him from the shoreline, "Cast your nets on the other side." The resulting catch of 153 fish caused Peter to leave the others and swim to shore. He knew the Master was waiting.

After eating the meal that the Lord had prepared, Jesus turned to the largest catch of fish that Peter would or could ever catch and asked, "Lovest thou me more than these," "Thou knowest that I love Thee," Peter replied "Feed my lambs." Then turning to him again Jesus asked the question. "Simon son of Jonas, lovest thou me?" Peter said, "Thou knowest that I love Thee," The Lord than said, "Feed my sheep." Then he asked again, possibly to receive one confirmation for each denial that Peter had spoken, "Simon son of Jonas lovest thou me?" With resolve in his voice Peter answered, "Thou knowest all things, Thou knowest that I love Thee, and Jesus said unto him "Feed my sheep."

Who are "His Sheep?" How do we feed them? Sitting in a virtual sea of people, the Lord had to send someone to remind me why I was there. It wasn't about forwarding my career. It wasn't about building a strong portfolio. It wasn't even about seeing the marvelous sights. It was about feeding "His lost sheep."

Once at the end of a church service, as the altar service began, a man made his way to the front of the church. As we were praying I realized that something was wrong and began to move toward him. As he stepped onto the platform I embraced him. Quietly, I asked him what he was doing and he said that he wanted to speak to the congregation. His breath revealed that he was well on his way to being drunk, so I coaxed him to the side of the auditorium where we could talk. The point of his intoxication was such that he believed he had super powers from God and could save the church. Knowing that God does not approve of confusion and it would harm those who could not know all the facts, I refrained from dragging him out the side door. Instead I insisted that the two of us pray together. Holding him firmly, so that he could not pull away and cause a scene, I began to pray. It was then that the Lord reminded me of the man who had grabbed my meal in New York City so many years ago.

As I prayed, I asked the Lord this question, "Is this the man you carried that cross for so willingly up Calvary's Hill? Is he the reason that you took all the stripes on your back? Is this the man that you died for?" And the answer came back to me with a resounding "Yes!" My prayer turned to tears as I held the man in my arms and prayed "Lord, please take back what the enemy has stolen here. Fix the things that are broken in his life. Repair the damage that sin has inflected and make this man, this man that you died for, make him whole and new again."

And then I prayed for myself, that I might be able to see through "His eyes" so that I will be able to see the things that He is trying to accomplish and not the things that I think should be done. There are many ways to cry, "Feed me, feed me." I need to be able to recognize the sound of that voice, no matter what the actual words are that are being used.

It is so easy to reach out for the clean, sober well-groomed people. People with respectable reputations are desirable candidates for His church. We are cautioned not to give a better seat in the house of God to someone wearing fine apparel, because we truly are all the same. Every child that is born is wonderfully and beautifully made and are equal in the eyes of God. It is after that point, as sin begins to tear away the natural beauty and leave scars on our lives that we become different to each other. Even though we may not feel completely comfortable in the presence of those who have destroyed their lives with sin, He is comfortable. Not that He loves the sin, but Jesus does love the sinner.

God is more than willing to sift through all the remaining pieces of a broken person's life in order to find something that He can restore and make whole again. His commandment was to "Feed my sheep," not to shear them.

In answer to the question Jesus asked, "Loveth thou me more than these," I don't ever want to put my career, my home, my bank account ahead of the things that God would want me to do. I pray that I will always remember the words of the man in Manhattan, "No, I want him to feed me." There was a song in one of our Christmas For Christ presentations a few years ago that Kay and I still remember and talk about. And in our mind's eye we can still recall the haunting pictures of people from every race and every walk of life as they sang, "Is That The Man Jesus Died For." Even though someone else may be willing or even more capable, I don't want anyone to take my place when Jesus says to me "Feed My Sheep."

Chapter Four

ARLO AND THE MIDNIGHT SAFARI

As the deafening roar of the firearm began to subside the sound of shattering glass filled the night. Arlo didn't even notice as he lowered his weapon. Checking to see if Herman was really dead, Arlo laid down the gun closed the top drawer of the chest and staggered back to his bedroom. Moments later he was sound asleep again, just as if nothing had really happened. Yet in the next room Herman lay dead, and next to him Emma knelt sobbing at her lost.

At one point in my life I became a good friend with a man named Arlo. Arlo had spent many years involved with friends who found their pleasures in the fantasy world created by narcotics. Now in the ladder years Arlo had abandoned that particular life style to pursue Christian

endeavors. And I had decided to try my hand at mentoring him as he grew in the faith. The scars of a hard life were evident and Arlo fought constantly to keep things balanced. And I might say he was doing a fairly good job of doing so, until Herman started hanging around his house. Not over jealous, Arlo was willing to put up with a whole lot, but everyone has their limits I suppose.

A lover of the outdoors Arlo spent a lot of time hunting and fishing thus neglecting some of the responsibilities you would normally expect the man of the house to take care of. As we have seen time and time again when you leave things unattended there is always someone waiting to move in and take your place. And for Arlo, Herman was the one trying to move in on his territory.

One spring Arlo had invited me over to go fishing with him on the river. He was especially excited about his new boat. This one was supposed to be newer, larger and considerably more stable that the canoe that he and I had clung to last winter as it went over the Dam in the swollen river near his home. The result of which was the near drowning the both of us. As you can see the invitation did cause me a certain amount of concern, but I did not want to offend him by refusing. A few weeks before Arlo had backed up his car while the door was open and sprung the hinge when the door hung on a passing tree. That day I had merely mentioned that he could put the handle of a sledge hammer that was leaning by the shed, in the door jam and gently push and it might spring it back in place. This suggestion being quickly turned down, I had sense enough to feel a storm coming in the immediate vicinity and made my excuses and left. It was later that when Emma saw her car and began to complain that Arlo lost it. "I heard Greg say that if you put the hammer handle in the door and close it, it will fix it," Emma had taunted.

"Fix it, fix it, I'll fix it," Arlo screamed as he thrust the sledgehammer in the doorway. Slamming with all of his strength Arlo slammed the door. Hitting the handle the door bounced open. Arlo slammed again. On the forth or fifth slam the passenger door of the late model sedan came completely off of the hinges and fell to the ground at Arlo's feet. Staring down disbelief at what he had done Arlo grabbed the door and slung it into the nearby hedgerow as Emma ran screaming and crying into the house.

For a while the word 'Greg' was not one spoken with fondness in Arlo and Emma's home. After several weeks of silence all had been forgiven and now Arlo had called inviting me to go fishing with him on his new boat. Somehow I had failed to catch the phrase 'On my new boat,' in the conversation and had thought he had meant in my new boat instead. Now arriving at the river, fishing gear in hand, ready to make amends. I stood speechless at the spectacle before me.

There, standing on the deck of his new boat, grinning from ear to ear stood Arlo. My first instinct was to get back in my truck and leave. But when you are really trying to get past some hard feelings you often let caution be tossed to the wind for the overall good of the relationship. 'The good ship Arlo" was yet another tribute to the uniqueness of its owner. The "new boat" was actually a 10' x 10' square raft. The raft was constructed of over 100 one-gallon plastic milk jugs. Each jug had its little lid tightly screwed on and was held in place by a piece of switch cane which was passed through its handle and tied with baling wire. The cane crisscrossed back and forth across the raft in a matte like pattern close enough to stand on without falling through. Tied to the matte in the middle of the raft were two lawn chairs. As I sat in one of the chairs and placed my tackle down beside me. Arlo took a long pole and pushed us out into the middle of the river where the current whisked us away.

It was a couple of hours later with water swishing in our shoes. As we were finally trudging up the game trail from the Forest to Arlo's back yard, that he finally spoke. " That wasn't so bad, If you would have just paid attention when I told you not to get near the edge it never would have happened. Besides we are getting pretty good at going over the dam, I hardly got any scratches that time. Why don't you come on in and we will dry out and maybe pop some popcorn.

It was when Arlo went into the bathroom that I saw Herman for the first time. As I turned my head from inspecting the interior of the refrigerator, I saw him slipping out of Emma's bedroom. "You dirty rat!" I screamed. "What are you doing here."

"What did you say?" Arlo called out from the other room.
 "Did you see the size of that rat?" I exclaimed.
"Oh, you must have seen Herman, "Emma replied. "He has been here for a few weeks and we can't seem to get rid of him. He eats the poison we put out like they are M&M's and lately he has been getting bolder and bolder. Now days he doesn't even run anymore when he sees us coming."

It was a week or so later as we were over at the Arlo's home that my wife got to see Herman. As we were finishing a wonderful meal that Emma had prepared Herman came walking out in the open area of the kitchen counter, he cut himself a slice of chocolate cake and calmly disappeared behind the toaster.

Not having learned my lesson in the past (the lesson being not to offer suggestions too freely around the Arlo's) I simply said. "My goodness Arlo that rat has gotten so big the only way that you are going to be able to get rid of it is to shoot the thing. Why I don't even know if that would do it. I'm not sure but I don't think that we have even killed any squirrels as big as he is, ha, ha, ha.

Emma only had one possession of any real worth.

Being as financially challenged as their family was did not

allow many luxuries. But the thing that meant most to Emma

was the china her mother had given her. These dished had

Chapter Five

BE CAREFUL HOW YOU BLESS ME

Lord be careful how you bless me, giving me more than I could hold.

If wealth will block my vision, how can I hope to see the goal?

I had a friend who served you faithfully, while poor and all alone.

Till one day you gave him riches, now his walk with you is gone.

I knew another who was dying, no strength left in him to give.

Spent all his hours in witnessing, telling others how to live.

With healing came the calling, of a world outside to know.

Now no one is left to tell the hurting, where to look or where to go.

There was a lady who was comely, and not yet in her prime.

Said you were all she needed, and with the children spent her time.

One day you gave her beauty, popularity then came too.

They no longer have a teacher, now who will tell them about you?

Lord, You know I want your blessings, More and more now every day.

If you will spread them through my life, so they won't cause me to stray.

If you hand them out too freely, or give me more than I need too.

I might find that I'm not man enough, to keep my eyes on you.

What would I profit then to gain the world, and in the end be cast away?

For life isn't worth living, unless you're in my life to stay!"

Chapter Six

SCARS ON MY FATHER'S HANDS

Surrounded by flames I began to scream in terror as the flames tore at my clothing.

As the nylon clothing began to melt to my skin, the crowd moved back and I turned and ran for the door. Without hesitation, my father tackled me and fell to the floor with me in his arms. With bare hands he began to beat out the flames. In my innocence, I thought he was spanking me for catching on fire. I didn't realize that he was trying to save my life.

Hours later as I came out from under the medication, I found that they had put me in the hospital. Looking across the room I saw him sitting silently by the bedside, tears of worry in his eyes. It was a while before I noticed that both his hands and arms were wrapped in heavy bandages. For a six year old, I had no idea how he had hurt himself and when I asked him what happened he simply shrugged it off and said, "It's nothing, how are you doing?" This I accepted and went on absorbed in my own pain, drifting in and out of consciousness throughout the night. It was the next day when a visitor came to my room and asked Mother how his burns were, that I realized for the first time that he had actually hurt himself trying to help me. It was then that I understood probably for the first time how much he really loved me.

My Dad worked Electrical Construction when I was growing up. He was a big burley giant of a man, hardly ever was sick and almost never got hurt. To hear him complain was a rarity. So that winter morning he came home from work in the middle of the day, bleeding from a wound across the side of his face caused quite a bit of excitement in our home. A piece of steel fell from somewhere up above him in a piperack and caught him on the jaw, knocking him to the ground. Rather than go to the doctor, he came home to treat the wound himself. As he stood at the bathroom mirror trying to shave his coarse beard away from the affected area so that he could apply a bandage, we all crowded around to watch in awe.

The small bathroom was not large enough for Dad, Mom and all five of us kids, yet we forced our way in. As each person jockeyed for position, I was soon pressed against the small gas space heater in the corner. Wearing a pair of nylon sweat pants and a tee shirt, it took only seconds before I went up in flames. And now lying in the hospital, I had thought that Dad was mad at me for catching on fire and that was the reason he had given me a spanking. But it had been an act of love.

My dad and I were never very close until after I was a grown man and I met my wife. They instantly hit it off and I began to see him through my wife's eyes and understand what a good man he truly was. It is funny that years later I found the scripture that said, "When I was a child, I spake as a child, I understood as a child, I thought as a child: but when I became a man, I put away childish things."

It also took until I was a grown man before I discovered Christ and His love. As I began my journey with my "Heavenly Father", I often did not understand His will for my life. Sometimes we think that God is punishing us, when in fact He is putting us in a position for our own good. Things that we look on as trials are the things that He allows to happen to us in order to save our lives. We have a heavenly Father who cares so much for our needs, that He didn't hesitate to come and sacrifice Himself for our salvation.

Once, I heard it said that the only thing in Heaven that is made by man, is the "scars in Jesus' hands." I hate that thought because it is true. The fact is that He loves us so much He would have done anything it took to insure that we could live with Him throughout eternity.

When Elijah was sitting by the brook and the Lord had the ravens feeding him daily, he felt the love of God. But when the brook dried up, he soon began to feel rejected, left out, forsaken and alone. But all alone, he was in the perfect will of God. He had prayed for it not to rain for three years and God honored that. As a result of no rain, it is a natural fact that the brooks and ponds would dry up. Yet God had already prepared a widow to take care of him.

He just had to allow the brook to dry up so that Elijah would get up and move to where God wanted him to be. And when later God moved him again for his own good, he hid in a cave and had a pity party. God himself then spoke to him and told him that he still had 70,000 followers left that had never bowed a knee to Baal. Elijah was not alone; God was just trying to take care of him.

It's sad that we so often let distance come between God and ourselves in our relationships to the point that when He tries to protect us we take it for punishment instead, but we do.

Never one time did I hear my Dad complain about the burns and then the scars on his hands. Yet I had complained extensively about my pain. A few years ago, I stood by his bedside as he was dying and I saw those scars still remained and in my heart there was absolutely no doubt about his love for me. How much more our "Heavenly Father" loved us. So much that He laid down His life for you and me.

1 Tim 3:16: *And without controversy great is the mystery of godliness: God was manifest in the flesh, justified in the Spirit, seen of angels, preached unto the Gentiles, believed on in the world, received up into glory.*

John 3:16: *For God so loved the world, that he gave his only begotten Son, that whosoever believeth in him should not perish, but have everlasting life.*

He loved us that much. . . I will never forget the "Scars On My Father's Hands."

Chapter Seven

THE NIGHT I KILLED NICHOLAS

Ha, Ha, Ha came the hideous laughter, just inches from my left ear. Turning quickly to my left, my heart nearly stopped as the small evil red squinty eyes stared at me from the darkness. Gripped in fear, I swung my right fist with all my might in the direction of my attacker. As my knuckles collided with his nose I was racked with pain, my hand feeling as if I had just hit a brick wall. Then to my disbelief his face exploded into a twisted collage of springs, wires and blinking lights, ending with a final ha, ha, ha. I stood trembling in the darkness holding my bleeding hand and feeling like a fool once again.

For a time, we lived in a very nice house in a beautiful neighborhood. This home was everything that I had ever dreamed of and I had wanted to stay there forever. We had not lived there very long however when things started to decline. At first it was little things, we would come home and find wet footprints around the swimming pool, indicating that someone had invited themselves over for a swim while we were gone. A couple of times a wolf whistle would penetrate the night when one of our household would pass close to a window late at night. Then things started to go missing. Little things at first, then increasing as time went on. Not normally a skittish person, I soon began to find this a more than a little unnerving. For example, on my birthday my wife bought me a beautiful cake for a surprise. This along with drinks, chips and dip for a surprise party she placed the birthday cake in the refrigerator, located in the garage area of our home. After church, she invited friends over and revealed the surprise. In the height of our festivities she went to retrieve the refreshments only to find that the cake along with all of the amenities were gone. Someone else had a birthday surprise of his or her own in mind.

It was a mid-December night when my wife first had shown me the motion sensitive talking Santa Clause Head she had found at the drugstore. It was cute, I had mumble as I continued to browse through my hunting magazine. There it was acknowledged, and that should have been the end of the subject. I wasn't paying much attention to where she was going to hang it anyway. I only watched for a few moments as she moved it from one place to another.

Two o'clock in the morning, a noise outside alerted us to the fact that we had a visitor. Once and for all I was going to catch this guy and put a stop to his pranks. Slipping out the side door of the house, I began to creep through the darkness. Balling my fist into tight hard weapons, I wasn't afraid of anything. Quietly I made my way between the car and the back door, ever so careful to listen and watch for any movement. The silence was so loud it was deafening. All I could heard was what sounded like someone loudly beating a drum wondering why the noise wasn't waking up the other neighbors, I realized that it was the beating of my heart that was making the sound, not a drum at all. Suddenly the stillness of the night was filled with the sound of the hideous laughter I mentioned earlier. Screaming from the top of my lungs (to frighten the enemy you understand) I went into action.

Now I'm standing here in pain, in the dark and cold trying to figure out how to tell my wife that I just killed old St. Nicholas. Granted, he hadn't been in the family very long, in fact I barely knew him. But none the less, I knew that she had already become attached to the little fellow.

Our house flooded this week and we lost a lot of things. During my exhaustion from all of the moving, cleaning, and throwing away I thought of Nicholas, and this is why. There were those who would call to offer their sympathy and make a token offer to help only to quickly find an excuse why they couldn't when I tried to accept their offer. I am most certainly not trying to indicate that some wonderful people did in fact not only offer to help but came bearing such items as carrot cakes and casseroles. And when they arrived rolled up their sleeves and worked alongside of us, and for that I will never forget them as long as I live. The thing is, I learned that when you are in the limb with the other hand. As weak as I was I couldn't reach it. One by one each finger gave up the struggle until only the smallest one was left. Try as it might it could not hold up my two hundred and plenty pounds of weight. So I launched into space.

I have come to realize so often we try to hold onto things that are not good for us. It is not that they are wrong for Christians to do or have. Many wouldn't even be considered a sin. It is just wrong for us to have them at this stage of our walk with God. As we try to hold on to them with one hand and our Christian walk with the other. The weight and distraction of these thing cause us to become to weak to recover until we find ourselves crashing to the ground. It could be a new toy (for some time I have been wanting a pontoon boat). The truth is I usually work during the week. This leaves weekends. Sundays are out.

Family holidays removed and your left with about forty Saturdays a year that you could use it. If you go boating every weekend your going to have marital trouble so that cuts it down to twenty times a year. Sixteen thousand dollars (a reasonable price for a boat) divided by twenty trips leaves each Saturday outing costing eight hundred dollars a day. I'm not that rich. The only other option would be to miss church on Sundays to go. That's only four hundred dollars a day (that's better).Now if I was to go in the middle of the week (Wednesday night) it would reduce it to two hundred and sixty six dollars a trip. Now it's getting more affordable. I know god loves me any way, and that's enough. Right?....Wrong !

This little example is exactly what I am talking about. Some things are hard to hold on to and live and work for God. Not long ago I found myself caught up in the world of toy collecting. As soon as I obtained a new toy, I was searching for the next awesome thing to buy before I even had time to play with the latest one. These things take up a lot of time. Time I could be using for the Lord's

work. Now, before the Ladies began to use this article to get their husbands attention, I would like to point out that we all seem to find too many distractions. It could be our jobs, our hobbies, music, close friends, automobiles, reading materials and the list goes on and on. The point is we really do try to hang on too to many things, that make it hard to hold onto Jesus.   I really must close now. I have just enough time to wash my motorcycle, tune up my three wheeler, sight in my compound bow, mount the new scope on my rifle, practice a new song on my guitar, load my scuba gear in the truck, paint the boat trailer, put up the volley ball net, clean the swimming pool and get to prayer meeting before I leave on vacation. Think about it!

Chapter Nine

NEVER TOO LATE

A shiver ran down my spine as I stepped out of the evening gloom and past the transient huddled in the doorway. I wasn't sure if I was shivering from the snow heaped along the sidewalk, the deteriorated condition of the high rise building or the task that awaited me somewhere on the third floor. I was more than just a little scared about what I was facing.

And now, after a routine day when I had settled in for the evening the phone call came. I had to answer the call. Now as I waited for the door to open, I whispered a quick prayer. Opening the door I was greeted by an older Spanish lady. She led me into a sparsely lit room seeming to understand when he folded my hands and said, "Pray for Bo." She smiled and nodded her head, then turned to lead me to the young man lying on the sofa. Then without a word she left the room.

At first appearance the frail form seemed lifeless, a mere shell of a man. Lackluster eyes blinked open when I spoke his name. Suddenly as if from nowhere the room began to fill with people. The introductions were made. Under the curious eyes of the quiet onlookers, boldness came over me and I began to speak possibly more to the crowd than to the man lying on the sofa." Bo Kenvessel's sister has called my Pastor all the way from Michigan and wanted someone from our church to come and pray for him. Bo, I understand is going back into the hospital tomorrow and the doctors have given him only a few weeks to live. Now before I pray, I want to tell you something about Jesus and what he expects from each of our lives. We don't want to just use God because we need something from him: He can be much more to us than that."

After giving a brief impromptu Bible study, I said those words I will never forget. "If anyone here doesn't believe that the Lord can touch this man, would you please leave the room while we pray." I had never said anything like that before in my life, and didn't quite understand why I felt impressed to say it now. With horror I watched as two men left their seats, then the room.

As suddenly as the boldness had come only seconds before, doubt arrived on the scene. The enemy began to whisper to Greg,

"You're not going to do any good. You're wasting your time. He has AIDS. No one has ever been healed from AIDS. You are only offering false hope."

After anointing Bo with oil, like the bible says. Everyone joined hands and began to pray. As I prayed, the Holy Spirit reminded me that I had been listening to the father of lies instead of the Heavenly Father. As I repented in my heart the anointing came and with it the sweet presence of the Lord. Tears fell through the crowd as I ministered to broken dreams and empty hearts. One by one all the remaining people stepped forward and ask me to pray for them. Each time I prayed the presence of the Lord would sweep through the room afresh. No one wanted to leave the room for to leave would be to walk out on God himself. After a couple of hours I excused myself somewhat in a daze, to reenter my own busy world. Amazed at the feeling of the Holy Spirit that I had felt in that simple prayer meeting

A few days after Christmas I visited the hospital and was told by the receptionist that Bo Kenvessel was no longer there. Assuming the worst, I had turned to leave as I contemplated the funeral. Interrupting my thoughts she said, "Wait, he was doing so well, we sent him home." I wanted to shout. Hurrying back the apartment building. I took the stairs two at a time. Upon knocking, a tall thin man whom I did not recognize answered my knock. It was our miracle! The skeletal frame had been replaced by a look of new strength. I had always believed that God worked miracles but I had never seen one with his own eyes. But here it stood right in front of my eyes. The questions that had been Building within me ever since receiving the news at the hospital erupted live an open flood gate. After much rejoicing Bo asked me to tell him more about Jesus.

During the weeks that followed I saw many wonderful things. Every bible study that I held at the Kenvessel's home would be filled with visitors. Friends family and many of other Aids infected people. I never had any idea who or how many would be present when I arrived. Never was I disappointed. Eventually the night came when Bo and most of his family attended the home mission church. I marveled at the way that God works. He had found a way to fill the Church that I would never have even considered possible.

Chapter Ten

WHEN SATAN TAKES YOU HOSTAGE

When Satan takes you hostage,
And you think that it's too late.
The call goes out, the ransom named.
And all you can do is wait
From peace you have been abducted,
Captive against your will.
Inside there is an empty feeling.
Through your soul there runs a chill.
Faith is bound, Cries are mute,
And your vision is blurred too.
Liberation seems so distance,
When reality comes crashing through.
Your Father is a rich man,
Owns the cattle of a thousand hills.
The enemy can only hurt him,
If a child of his they steal.
But Jesus will never forsake you,
He's already paid the fee.
From the moment you were captured,
He sent angles to set you free.
He's had the place surrounded,
And everything is in control.
In the shadows he only is waiting,
Until you seek refuge for your soul.
When he hears your cry the bonds are broken.
A Heavenly Calvary comes rushing in.
Like a brilliant sunrise in the morning,
Grace begins for you again.

Chapter Eleven

WHO'S AFRAID OF THE BIG BAD WOLF?

"Seeing him lying there on the ground, his hair matted and covered in mud, chains on every foot, I was no longer afraid".

As I pulled the covers over my head and trembled with fear yet one more time I kept trying to tell myself I was safe. And I was, only a ten-year-old boy doesn't have much past history to rely on so everything seemed more intensified. Night after night I could hear them outside. Howling at the moon, calling to each other and growing closer and closer to our house as the night wore on. Timber Wolves, big wild dogs that roamed the nearby woodlot by night and disappeared during the day. I had seen their tracks in the sand by the creek; they were huge. And day by day knowing that they were out there somewhere my fear had grown until I was almost sick. I didn't want to go out and play any longer with my friends. I just wanted to hide under the covers.

The night came when the wolves broke into my neighbor's rabbit cages and devoured the helpless prey. I saw their trail of destruction and with tears in my eyes asked my dad what could we do. Later that evening a friend of my dad's came over with a large burlap sack full of steel traps. I watched with wonder as he set trap after trap in a maze around the barnyard. That night I could hardly sleep with excitement knowing that those traps might catch the seven foot tall, thousand pound, fire breathing, teeth glistening, hot breath, slobber dripping, demons of the darkness, "The Wolves".

Years later, long after I was a grown man I encountered another pack of dogs. These were coyotes and we were camping in east Texas on Lake Sam Raburn with a group of young men from the church. As night fell a group of the dogs gathered outside the camping complex and began to howl at each other announcing their arrival. Already in my tent I could not help but over hear the talk of those remaining around the campfire. By their conversation it was apparent that they were unnerved by the sound of the uninvited guest at out camp. Having gotten over my fear of the wild beast years ago I could not help but laugh at their concern.

Those around the fire made the decision to take turns all night staying up to keep a big fire burning to keep away the coyotes

Chapter Twelve

GREEN IS NOT MY COLOR!

This is really gonna hurt bad after a while! On a night when I really should have been at choir practice with my wife, I had to work. Well…sort of. Deer season was almost here and I hadn't built a new deer stand.

Drilling a piece of metal, the drill motor hung up and spun the sharp metal like a propeller, with my hand in its path. In a state of shock, I examined my hand. There was a deep cut across the palm and the thumb was ripped from top to

bottom. I decided maybe I didn't need a new deer stand this year. Searching through the medicine cabinet, I soon found all the things I needed for the repairs. Not having children, there were not many items for patching cuts and scrapes, but I did find the basics. Armed with hydrogen peroxide, cortisone crème, gauze, and tape I went to work. Having used all the above supplies and being quite proud of myself, I retired for the evening.

In a misdirected attempt to solicit sympathy from my wife when she came home, I gingerly placed my injured hand on her pillow and went to sleep. I awoke to find my wife standing over me waving a bottle of alcohol in her hand explaining that she was sure I had not done an adequate job of dressing the wound. Traumatized by the sight of the "giant" bottle of alcohol, I could not bear to witness the procedure and turned to face the wall. Only after the cleansing of my hand did she discover, I had used all the gauze and tape, so back to the medicine cabinet she went. Later when my hand was released to my care, I quickly shoved it under the covers and breathed a sigh of release and went back to sleep.

Hours later, in the quiet of the night my hand began to throb painfully. Lifting my hand from beneath the covers, I gasped in horror at what I saw. Breathlessly, I tried to call out to my wife. "Kay, wake up, you're not going to believe this," but to no avail. She was sound asleep. I had to face this problem alone. There, right before my very eyes, to my disbelief my throbbing hand was glowing in the dark! It was neon green and glowing in the dark! Now, it really hurt! Just like I had seen in the comics, it was glowing brighter and brighter by the moment. I knew then, even if it was three o'clock in the morning that I needed to call my pastor. But gaining some control of my faculties, I made my way to the bathroom and found the light switch and turned it on.

As suddenly as my situation came, with the coming of light, the problem was gone. The word problem, by the way, is not found in the Bible. There, covering my hand was what had to be a half a box of "Glow In The Dark" Band-Aides. Who knew that they even made such a thing? Much less the fact that we had some in our home. My wife had let our nephew, Cheston, pick them out. Oh, blessed relief! Immediately, the word of God came to me. "God is light, and in Him is no darkness at all." Another place says, "He will bring to light the hidden things of darkness." We are instructed to walk as children of light. As His children, if we would always bring our needs to Jesus and let Him shine His light on them, we would soon begin to realize, that like the Bible, we have no "problems" at all.

Chapter Thirteen

WHEN YOU GET THERE BEFORE GOD DOES

"A few years ago there was a man who attended our church whose hobby was skydiving. He just loved to jump out of airplanes. Now, I never could understand just why someone would want to jump out of a perfectly good airplane while it was still working, but he did. In fact, he and a couple of his friends went together and bought an airplane, just so that they could jump out of it two or three times a week. Like I said, I thought it was a foolish thing to do, but they really seemed to enjoy it.

One Sunday morning he came to church and told me, "I had a malfunction yesterday." And he seemed happy about it. "What did you do?" I asked. "When my chute didn't open, I just relaxed, I took a deep breath, thought about what they taught us in jump school. So I pulled my emergency rip cord and drifted safety down to earth."

"Weren't you scared," I asked him. "No, that was the neatest part of the whole thing. I always thought that I would be, but I wasn't. I knew what I was supposed to do and I did it. And it worked, it was great." It didn't seem great to me. I could not see how any malfunction could be a good one. A few weeks later he came by and told me about a competition sport dive where they had just jumped. They were trying to break the records by forming a fifty-man connected star at several thousand feet in the air. When he told me what had happened on that jump, I thought that it was one of the most spectacular things that I had ever heard of.

These guys had trained and planned and rehearsed for weeks. Everything was ready, and then the day came. Cameramen, coaches, jumpers and alternates, all climbed into their planes, and jumped into the history books. One by one the people drifted into their position and the star began to take shape. Due to the changing glide ratio and wind resistance, the speed at which the jumpers were falling began to decrease as each new member joined the group. They actually became a glider.

Skydiving is supposed to be simple, in that you merely point yourself in the direction you want to go and you begin to move forward and (down) in that direction. Individual jumpers fall much faster than the overall group and have to time their jump in order to reach their position correctly. They also had alternate jumpers as a part of that group. In the event that someone missed their mark and fell away. There would be someone to ready fill their empty place in the star.

In his haste to make his lifelong dream complete, one of the jump leaders came in too fast and missed his position. Falling much faster than the others, it soon became apparent that there would be no way he could become an effective part of the group. Everything that he had worked for would be lost. Knowing from experience that he could trust his emergency chute he made a decision. Turning to get out of the path of the other jumpers he opened his parachute. This slowed his decent until the others fell past him. Then he purposely collapsed his own chute and cut it away. He then began to freefall until he reached the safety of the group and filled the position that was needed. He did this with confidence, because he knew that he still had the protection of his emergency chute to bring him safely home.

People who step out in front of the group are called leaders. Leaders do not do great things simply because they are leaders. Rather, great men are leaders because they do great things. Simply deciding that we want to take an active part in the Church leadership does not qualify us as leaders. The Bible does say however, "whom God calls he qualifies." It is the few who are willing to turn loose of the secure things in order to see the Church become all that it can be that are the true leaders.

When we find that we face a malfunction in our walk with God, or even get to the place where no one even understands our intentions, and you will, or maybe things are happening to fast to control and it seems like all you can do is hang on. It doesn't mean that our vision is unobtainable. It just calls for extreme actions. The few who are willing to trust God when all hope seems gone, these are the ones that can properly fill the positions that God has appointed. Moses had a Red Sea to cross with the enemy at his back, and then to top it all off a storm came. But he still stepped out in faith ahead of the group. Elijah had to find his way out of a cave. Joshua's ministry looked like it was just walking around in circles. Jacob had to wrestle an angel to get a blessing from God. Samuel lost a night's sleep and made a few false starts, before he finally even found out what God wanted him to do. But the main thing is every person who is effectively used of God gets their strength from time spent alone with God away from the group.

It's during this time that we learn that we to have an "emergency chute." One that will slow our decent until the plan of God comes back into view. Then we simply have to point ourselves in the direction we need travel and move forward in that direction. Then God's perfect will once again comes within our reach.

No one can fill your position as well as you can when God ordains it. The scripture tells us *'Let us not be weary in well doing. For in due season we shall reap, if we faint not.'* When many of the great men of God first saw their plans and dreams escape their grasp, I was hard to believe that their ministries would flourish again. Many even doubted that they could even be effective for God in a small way. We know that God works in special time frames that often we don't understand. But, unless we time our ministries to work in his plan, we are often left holding nothing but thin air. With that realization, we often panic and give up. But, Ben it doesn't have to be that way. So often we see good people spiritually destroyed, simply because they failed in some endeavor. As long as we live we can always be used of God as long as we keep on trying. When things seem to be going wrong, and they will, just don't panic. It's just a malfunction. It is not over.

Chapter Fourteen

DID YOU SAY CHICKEN SNAKE?

The sitar music played softly in the background, trying to see through opiate smoke, I turned away from the worshipers still bowing as they kneeled on the floor. With the sound of their praise fading away I stepped through the beaded curtain into the next room. Suddenly I froze where I stood, there on the floor in the center of the room; sitting on a white fur rug was a young beautiful blond haired woman wearing a Boa Constrictor Snake. As she rubbed the snake's head across her cheek she sang softly and gently placed kisses on his head with loving tenderness.

Did I ever mention that I was terribly afraid of snakes? Well I am it goes all the way back to when I was a small boy playing in the dirt next to the roots of a tree near the barn yard. Thinking I was hearing one of grandma's geese hissing at me I turned on my knees to swat the pesky bird away. To my horror I was staring eye level, face to face just inches away from a coiled and ready to strike cottonmouth moccasin. I did manage an escape, but the effect was terminal. Even today over forty years later, with as much as I love the outdoors I still melt with fear when I first see a snake.

I once worked with a man who walked with a limp, he told me he had been drinking one evening and upon leaving the bar saw a rattle snake crossing the road and decided to have some fun. Catching the snake he pored a large portion of whisky down the snake's throat trying to get the snake drunk. Having done so he put the snake back on the ground and turned it loose. He said he wanted to see how a snake would act drunk. The moment the snake was free it turned on him and bit him on the leg just below the knee. Now years later after he almost lost the use of his leg, the knee was stiff and would no longer bend. His drinking buddy had turned on him.

Several times I have narrowly escaped being bitten by the reptiles while in the wild. Once my brother in law Mark shot a snake that was coiled to strike just inches from my leg. While I was still in the air descending from the jump caused by the initial reflex action upon hearing him holler, "look out! Snake!" He fired and killed it leaving me to land in a pile of various assorted snake parts. I was sure he had tried to blow away my kneecaps.

The word of God tells us to …"Flee the very appearance of evil." We need to be able to recognize sin for what it is and be prepared to flee as soon as we see it. Let us always be conscious of the results of our actions.

The skin and texture of a snake is so appealing that in our culture People make clothes, shoes purses and belts out of it to wear for decoration. God forbid that we see the beauty in sin and decorate our lives with it. We need to mark it for what it is and leave it alone. Our actions should always indicate that we are afraid of the results of sin.

And that when it comes to the earthly reptiles as well, we are chicken when it comes to snakes!

Chapter Fifteen

DOES "BUFFALOED" MEAN CONFUSED?

As soon as his friends and family realized that he was injured, they quietly surrounded in an effort to support him simply by their presence. With troubled looks on their faces, no one spoke. They only continued to stare. Then, as if on command, several members of the group closed in tight and sandwiched him between them.

It seemed that their intent was to protect him from further sniper fire. But the presence of the entire group was accomplishing that. By pressing in close, they were actually holding him up on his feet. They refused to let him fall.

Only after what seemed like an unbelievable amount of time did they begin to grow weary and finally let him slip to the ground. Then to the amazement of the onlookers, two of the stronger Bulls lowered their heads. One on either side of their now dying companion and started to lift him back to his feet. For about a half an hour these two determined individuals struggled and worked to lift him. Often they would actually get him into a sitting position, only to have him topple once more to the ground. When totally exhausted, they joined the rest of the group who maintained their silent vigil, refusing to leave. After several hours, Richard Kohler and his friends had to use two large farm tractors to disperse the protective herd on their upstate Michigan Buffalo Ranch. I am told that this type of teamwork is often seen in this remarkable species. All my life I have heard the expression "that buffaloed me," when something is found to be confusing. Now, I'm not so sure that is a correct statement. It seems to me that we as the Church, could learn a few lessons from the Bison. When we see one of our own brothers or sisters in the Lord hurting, struggling and wounded, we should rush immediately to them. To recover, they may need our strength to support them. So often, we actually run to disassociate ourselves from the hurt and wounded. We don't want to become involved, possibly receive a blemish to our name or give of ourselves. Those incredible buffalo actually held up their dying companion until there was no more life left in him. Still yet, they held him. Elders upon seeing him laying there, even tried to lift him back to his feet by force. When was the last time that we went after the spiritually sick and wounded to find out what happened to them or to try to bring them back into the arms of God? We have become so comfortable in our padded pews that we have ourselves believing that we are the ones being rejected by them and we get our feelings hurt. Possibly thinking that they didn't like our preaching or our music, when in reality they are facing a spiritual warfare that we can't even begin to comprehend and are swiftly losing.

If the mere Buffalo can accomplish such an awesome feat as this, it should be the responsibility of every blood-bought Christian to reach out and minister to the wounded whenever and wherever we find them. By faith, I know we can "Stand In The Gap" for them.

The above story, about the buffalo's unique behavior, was related to G. Bullock by Richard Kohler, who reported that this happens quite frequently among buffalo herds.

Chapter Sixteen

LORD WE NEED TO TALK

Lord we need to talk.

It's just occurred to me.

Most of the time we spend together,

Is when you come to rescue me.

I don't take the time to listen, Until troubles slow me down.

Then urgently I seek you,

While fear still has me bound.

You have always been so faithful,

To cast out my despair.

When thanks you's pass with praise forgot,

You still act on all my prayers.

I know I stay way too busy,

With things that fill my day.

While your still reaching from the background,

I turn and walk away.

Until now it's been a week relationship,

If I'm to continue things must change.

The way it is I only seek you out,

To help me ease the pain.

The past has been established,

I can't change one moment or one deed.

Guilt can't carry me through tomorrow.

It's your companionship I need.

Until now I have been doing all the talking,

Stopping by when I need a friend.

From now on I'll try to listen,

And begin with you again.

Chapter Seventeen

THE TRIBAL DANCE OF THE HAIRY-NECK MUD STOMPER

Quite often I find myself in strange situations that are so completely unique. I am positive that my Nut-Magnet powers are at work once more. I have to wonder how do I attract these people?

It seemed like a perfectly normal day when it started out. Daylight found me ankle deep in mud, shivering from the cold, deep in the forest on a hunting expedition. And I thought life doesn't get any better than this. The fresh smell of the new fallen Pine needles, the sound of birds chirping, the cackle of a flock of geese as they passed overhead below the cloud cover. Suddenly I heard a terrible growling sound; griped with fear I knew I better act fast. I started for my truck to make the long drive to town. With the growling of my empty stomach growing louder with each step. I knew I had to find a restaurant and in a hurry.

Arriving in a small rural community I quickly spotted the only restaurant that appeared to be open and hastily parked on the nearly empty parking lot and headed for the doorway.

Upon reaching the door I happened to notice that my shoes were covered with mud. Not wanting to soil the floor I decided to take the time to try to clean my shoes before I entered. As I turned away and started to walk down the short incline ramp leading to the entrance I noticed a young man start toward the door. Seeing me he stepped back and out of my way. Stepping to the side I began to stomp my foot in order to dislodge the mud from my boot.

Turning away from the ramp I stomped my right foot. Then I heard a sound (stomp). I then stomped my left foot, again a sound (stomp). Turning back to face the man I stomped my right foot twice. Again (stomp, stomp) the man mimicked. So then I did a quick right foot double (stomp) followed by a left foot (stomp). Just to see if he was taunting me. Immediately came the answer, right foot (stomp, stomp), left foot (stomp). I took a step back; He took a step back. Right foot (stomp), left foot (stomp, stomp), right foot (stomp). He did a right foot (stomp), left foot (stomp, stomp), right foot (stomp).

Now he was starting to bother me more than just a little. I didn't know if we were doing the hokey-pokey or what. I was expecting him to start flapping his arms up and down like a pair of wings at any second. Circling him like two roosters about to fight I did another quick (stomp, stomp) just to be counteracted once more. I was beginning to feel as if I was involved with in some sort of ritualistic tribal dance. Had I violated some sacred custom? Here I was doing the "Tribal Dance of the Hairy Neck Mud Stomper" and I didn't even know why. Raising my hands to defend myself I challenged him." Hey have you got some kind of problem here, I'm just cleaning the mud from off of my shoes before I go inside."

Twisting to and fro like a man trying to escape from a strait jacket he looked me in the eye. "Yea, I got a problem!" he blurted out. The challenge was accepted my heart froze at the thought of the ensuing altercation about to come. As I was preparing for the fight he spoke again. "I just came out of that barbershop across the street and I got hair all down the back of my neck and it's itching. I thought by stomping like you were I might dislodge some of it."

With relief I smiled at my dancing partner and went on in the restaurant (of course I kept an eye on him across the room as I cautiously ate my meal). The whole ordeal unnerved me to the point that I even left my glasses in the restaurant upon my departure and had to return later to retrieve them. As I drove away I had to ask the question I have asked so many times in the past. "OK Lord, what was it you wanted me to see this time.

The answer came on Sunday evening during the song service in church. Not everyone has the same relationship with Jesus. Everyone's problems are different, and yet we try to resolve our problems based on the methods we have seen others use as opposed to asking the Lord himself what he would have us to do. Often we hear people say, "Well Brother Doohickey doesn't do it that way. Why should I." Or, Sister Whatzhername does this and she always seems to be blessed. Why should I have to be the one who has to do all the sacrificing all the time." And then we wonder why God doesn't answer our prayers by removing us from our discomforting situations.

Here is a thought, why don't we just ask God what he would have us to do instead of trying to get someone else to read the

This list could go on and on, but we shouldn't fall captive to this trickery. The word of God gives us a peace with the scripture. "Take therefore no thought for the morrow: for the morrow shall take thought for the things of itself. Sufficient unto the day is the evil thereof." Matt. 6:34.

Jesus tells us that by worrying we cannot increase our height nor add hair to our head and that instead of seeking food and clothing we are to seek first the kingdom of God. And then, all these other things will be added to us. In an effort to be wise stewards with the monies the Lord has entrusted to us, and in an effort to live the Christian life in public that we proclaim we have, we often put many undue pressures on our families and ourselves. All the while fearing public failure. Once again the enemy uses his favorite tool to take what we mean to be responsible, and uses it to try and destroy our walk with God. We need to realize that worry and fear are both physically and spiritually unhealthy and have no fellowship with Jesus.

Sitting in my deer stand on that quiet morning several years ago. I saw a small rabbit literally have a nervous breakdown, which led to his own demise. For lurking in the tall swamp grass nearby was a large bobcat just waiting for someone to believe that escape was not an option. If we would just learn to "resist the devil ... he will flee." We shouldn't be the ones that are afraid, Satan trembles when he sees even the weakest Christian on his knees. Just think of the response that we can evoke when someone strong in faith begins to pray.

Chapter Nineteen

THE WRONG ADDRESS...THE RIGHT NIGHT

As I walked away from the car, stumbling through the dark,
I was worried about the neighborhood and where I had to park.
I tripped on an object hidden in the grassy parking lot.
To my disgust, I tore my suit and bruised my pride somewhat.
This is not the way it was supposed to happen!
Where were the crowds I came to see?
The invitation that came in the mail, said this was the place to be.
I came just early enough to make an appearance, with little time to
pray.
After all I was the speaker, I walked with God throughout the day.
When I spoke, they came to listen and paid a hefty fee.
If anyone wanted to know more about God, they naturally came to
me.
I stepped over the piece of broken siding lying on the walk
and at my touched the railing came loose. Me and someone would
have a talk!
As I climbed the faded steps towards the peeling stain glass door,
it seemed the place was abandoned and no one came here anymore.
The door creaked loudly open and I smelled the damp stale air.
I knew I had the "wrong address," this revival could go nowhere.
I could tell this Church had had its good times and had served its
purpose well.
There were tear stains on the altar, where men had escaped the
bonds of hell.
The song books were old and tattered and most of the covers now
were gone.
Their backs were badly broken, pages dog-eared at favorite songs.
In the corner was the Baptistery, eaten up with rust.
It was once the center of attention, but was covered now with dust.
Its working days were over and could never be used again.
Once a very useful tool, to bury the sins of men.
Coming to the platform, I felt the boards give beneath my feet.
Then came a sense of sadness, no it felt more like defeat.
I thought of all the hopes and dreams, this place had surely borne
and wondered if its passing had caused anyone to mourn.

Right on to the pulpit, my feet did take me next.
By an uncontrollable urging, my soul was sorely vexed.
Standing behind that mighty desk, decayed wood clutched in my hands,
the strangest thing did happen, I'll never understand.
The piano in the corner, began to play so slow and soft,
"Thank God For The Blood" or was it "The Old Rugged Cross?"
The melody that it beckoned, unimportant now it seems.
For no sooner had it started, than I thought it was a dream.
Through the back door came the people, a vision out of time.
One by one they took their places, I thought I'd lost my mind.
As they began to worship, the power of God fell once more.
I tried to speak but couldn't, for I'd seen this scene before.
From the street there came a young man, tall and in control.
His back was straight, his face was set, but there was trouble in his soul.
His heart was badly broken and his youth ravaged by sin.
Life to him was a disappointment, there were no such things as friends.
Faith to him was fiction and hope just another word.
To trust again...out of the question unless the voice of God was heard.
His face looked so familiar, though I couldn't really tell.
The sins that he had covering him, were dragging him toward hell.
To the front he didn't come, but knelt in the back to pray.
From the fire around the altar, he tried to stay away.
But the fire itself was catching, sweeping through the room.
A purging fire from God above, seeking sins to consume.
The room went strangely quiet, until only one voice I heard.
Pleading for his mortal soul, with barely audible words.
With a groaning from his very being, the man began to cry.
My God, my God, have mercy on a sinner such as I.
Then I saw it happen, his life was made complete.
He finally gave it all to God, laid it at his Savior's feet.
Then to my amazement, a different man arose.
A fiery chill ran through my body, from my head down to my toes.
As he made his way down to the front, I could clearly see.
The man who gave his heart to God, was a much younger "Me."

What have I been thinking, what is wrong with me?
I was only just a sinner, until Jesus set me free!
Now the years and time have past, until I'd gotten to a place
where I had thought God came to me,
to help judge the human race.
My opinions I have offered, whether welcomed they would be
and said I'll teach you how to grow, if you'll just listen to me.
But suddenly things are different, I've finally broken free.
For the revival that I came to hold, had gotten a hold on me.
I didn't even mind the dust, as I fell headlong to the floor.
This prodigal son had come home again, to follow God once more.
I laid there and I talked to God, we talked the night away.
He would talk and I would listen, when I arose it was breaking day.
When I stepped out in the morning light and walked back to my
car,
the whole world looked new again, without a spot or mar.
I was going home a different man, though my appearance looked
the same.
There never was a revival, where I was more glad I came.
Then driving down the highway, I was amazed to see,
that just ahead two exits, there was a large marquee.
With neon lights still flashing, the promise of last evenings events,
"REVIVAL, REVIVAL, A MAN FROM HEAVEN SENT!"
The sign gave the promise, with faith and healing I would be there.
I wondered about the people, did I truly care?
Had I come to reach them? To help save their mortal soul
or was it all about numbers, is that where I'd lost control?
As I drove on past the exit, I thought I'd go back home,
when somewhere in my journey, I passed a man who was alone.
I could tell that he was homeless, his youth had been long spent.
Searching through the garbage, his back was frail and bent.
His dreams had long been stolen, the world just passed him by.
I tried in haste to reach him. Then he began to cry,
"I'm tired of your self-righteous, taking pity on me.
You don't want to help, it's your conscience you want to set free."
His words hit me like an axe, a deadly blow did fall.
His words were words of truth, did he matter to me at all?
I really had to stop and think, just what to me was love?

If I didn't get to know the man, how could I tell him about God above?

It was one thing to hide behind a desk and preach to others about heaven.

But another thing altogether, to sit and listen to people, your time having

given.

You see people are more than numbers.

Crowds are made it seems of people standing together with people,

each having their own dreams.

A crowd won't go to heaven, there's no discount or group plan.

No one person can pay another man's way, alone before God he'll have to stand.

So in order to be a man of God and do his perfect will,

I must first become a friend of man, a relationship to build.

If in my heart I can't find a place, to take some time with them,

then I'm not who I say I am and I'm not true to Him!

I've been way to busy, rushing to and fro,

advising theologians, not allowing myself to grow.

I'd like to stop and visit, to take time to tell you more.

But with their lives in shambles, are people broken, tired and sore.

I'm going now to be a friend to them, no matter what the cost.

For if I don't take the time to care, then I myself, may be lost!

Chapter Twenty

CHANGE FROM CHAINS

Falling end over end, the whole world was spinning out of control. The horizon was a blur as it would come into view and then out again. Helplessly he fought to gain control. With each passing second the ground grew closer and closer. There was no way to avoid the fatal crash. In desperation he cried out for his father to save him. . . . . .

Yesterday, his world had been perfect. Living in his parents home, he had it made. It was warm, comfortable; he had everything that he needed. A soft bed to sleep in, a hot meal every time he had asked and most of all a family that loved him. Never had he been alone, always one of his parents had been with him. The home was filled with love and devotion. And then it happened. . .

Without any explanation, his parents had come home and put him out of the house.

As he watched, they threw his soft furry bed away and withdrew from his presence. Every time he tried to draw close to them, they would scold him and chase him away. He could not understand what was going on. What had happened? He knew that he had done nothing wrong and yet he suddenly was being treated as if he had become a stranger.

Approaching night brought with it a cold drizzling rain and overwhelming grief. After wandering about in tears for what seemed liked hours, he finally found shelter under the overhang of a rock. All night long he trembled from the cold and fear. He cried until tears came no more. Afraid to sleep for fear that the nightmares would increase; he waited for the coming morning. As the sun rose over the nearby mountain top and began to share its warmth, he was surprised to see his father standing there watching him. Afraid it was just a vision, he did not move. Finally his father called out to him. Then slowly his father came to him and embraced him. It was hard to believe that he was really there.   It felt good to be in father's arms again. It was warm, it smelled good, he felt the strength, and he felt the love. He just wanted to be able to go home. Thinking he was taking him home, he let his father help him up on his back to carry him away.

Duet 32:11 As an eagle stirreth up her nest, fluttereth over her young spreadeth abroad her wings, taketh them, beareth them on her wings: So the lord alone did lead him, and there was no strange god with him He made him to ride on the high places of the earth, that he might eat the Increase of the fields: and he made him to suck honey out of the rock, oil out of the flinty rock:

The trial that you are going through may be a miracle in the birth process; Jesus said that he would never leave you nor forsake you. Just wait until you see what happens next.

Suddenly only moments before crashing into the ground. The adult eagle swooped down and caught the young bird upon his back, and started toward heaven once more. This continued again and again until finally upon one magic moment the young bird's wings filled with air and he himself began to soar upward. It has been said over and over again,

"You can never fall faster than your Father can fly!"

The eagle is the only bird equipped to fly above the storms. Others have to wait them out in misery, but the eagle has the power to soar above them, but first he must learn to fly. If the young eagle had never experienced the change from the chains that kept him earth bound he would never had been able to rise above the storms that came his way.

As change takes place in your life look forward with expectation to the places that God is trying to take you. You can never fall faster than My God can Fly!

Chapter Twenty One

GOOD GOLLY MISS MOLLY

I always wondered what it would be like to wake up one morning and find that someone had left a baby on your front doorstep. Well here goes….I never can seem to do things the normal way.

Being held hostage in a sandbox is not how I had planned to spend my Saturday. I remember thinking, I wish David Parsons were here. I promised him I would include him the next time something like this happened. With me in the sandbox was Molly. We were building sandcastles. Not exactly what a middle-aged man with a 24' pontoon boat and a pile of scuba gear would normally want to be doing on a beautiful morning in June. But on the other hand, Molly was a real looker. Long blond hair, blue eyes and petite. . .oh, and did I mention she was 6 years old? I am afraid we didn't have a lot in common. On the other hand, I was learning a lot about building sandcastles.

"Where is Molly!" her mother screamed. "I thought she was with the other children when they climbed into your car." "No! **Came the anguished reply.** *"I thought you had her, we must have left her at the last house we stopped at and that's a half hour away!"*

Earlier I had finished trimming the hedges on the side of the house and waved at my neighbor and her friends as they climbed into their vehicles and drove away. From the way they were dressed, it was easy to tell that they were headed for a fun-filled day at the beach. As I gazed at all the little kid's heads appearing in each window, I was thankful that I didn't have the responsibilities that was associated with chaperoning a group that size.

Suddenly, I heard the sound of a small child screaming in terror. As the scream subsided into uncontrollable sobbing, I dropped what I was doing and rushed in the direction of the sound. I could not believe my eyes at what I saw.

There standing all alone, wearing a black swimsuit laced with red and yellow flowers holding a beach towel was a tiny little blond haired girl. I knew the answer even before I ask, "What's the matter honey?"

"They left me! I was doing what Mommy said. She told everyone to go use the bathroom before we left, and when I came out they had left me…….." and the sobs began again.

"It will be OK," I tried to reassure her. "When they find out you're missing, they'll come right back and get you. Your Mom would never leave you alone for long."

As she began to calm down she started talking. "We were going to my favorite beach so I could build sand castles. It's my favorite thing to do. And now I won't get to go, because they left me."

Still trying to calm her down, I tried to get her to let me take her to my house where my wife Kay was and while she consoled her, I could make some phone calls. Firmly she told me, "No! I'm not supposed to go anywhere with strangers."

"Please!"

"No!" Ok I thought I will try something else, "Let's just go over there and stand in my yard where I can watch you out the window while I go inside and make some phone calls.

"No! I'm not supposed to cross the street."

"Come on, please!" What am I supposed to do? I don't have any little children, so what do I do now, I wondered. "Come on sweetheart be a sport."

"I said No!" I am not supposed to go anywhere. And beside that I when I am lost I am supposed to stay right where Mommy left me until she comes back, that way she will know where to find me.""

"But if you come with me we can get you some help."

"No! I m not going!"

"Ok then we will just stay here in the yard until she comes back," I said.

With that she began to tear up again. "Oh no, I 'm not supposed to go outside and play unless I am with a babysitter and I don't have a babysitter. "I'm going to be in real trouble."

I seemed to remember everyone thinking the movie "Home Alone" was really funny. By this time, I was beginning to fail to see the humor of the situation. "I'll be you baby sitter," I said.

"But I don't know you," she sobbed.

"I am a good guy you little twerp or I wouldn't be wasting my time trying to help you. Now you get yourself right across that street like I said or I'll drag you over myself. Now march it left, right, left, right…." Man I wanted to say that so badly. But what if she started to scream again? There is so much child abuse going on in this country another passerby could have me arrested thinking I was attacking her. "Oh Lord, what am I supposed to do?" I asked, I just wanted to trim my hedges this morning. I didn't ask for any of this. Bending slightly at the waist, I put on my best smile and said. "I'm Mr. Greg and I live in that house right there, I said pointing to our house." I am a good friend with Mr. and Mrs. Neighbor who live right here in this house. And I want to be your friend. What is your name?'

"Molly."

"How old are you?"

"Six and a half."

"Wow you sure are big for six and a half. Do you go to school yet? After a long time of indecision she finally relented and we began to become acquainted. Looking around the neighbor's yard I spotted a sandbox and led Molly to it and suggested that she build me a sandcastle while we waited.

After what seemed like hours, phone in her hand, my wife rushed from our house, "Had I found a little girl?" she asked. Molly's mom had discovered that she was gone and our neighbor had called us. A reassuring phone call, a promise to be there soon and everyone was fine. A few minutes later, a friend of Molly's mom rushed over from around the block to comfort her and stay with her until mom got back. And as quick as the situation arrived at my door, it was over. "I wonder why I had to be the one to find her," I thought as I went back to my hedge trimming.

Two o'clock in the morning I awoke wide-awake in my bed and the Lord spoke to my heart. The question was "What was it I learned from Molly?"

"Molly what do you mean? Molly was a little girl what could she teach me?" Then I began to see it all differently and here is what I learned from Molly -

I'm not supposed to go anywhere with strangers - meaning "*I may be lost but I not stupid.*"

I'm not supposed to cross the street – meaning " *Say whatever you want but I'm not leaving where I am supposed to be* "(polite, but firm).

I'm not supposed to be outside without a baby sitter – meaning, *"If I go outside I better have someone watching over me."*

Mommy will come back and get me- and when she does I am going to be right where I am supposed to be.

If only we could be like Molly: Maybe we are having the worst day of our life, things are going wrong. All the dreams we have tried to build are crumbling like sandcastles. We are scared and confused, but there is no reason to leave the instructions we are taught from God's word. We don't need to blame God for our problems. He wants us to do good. He is still coming back and when he does, we need to be where we are supposed to be. He has sent a comforter to be with us, to protect us and to guide us until His return. Just because things are going wrong, we shouldn't turn our backs on God. His rules are the same in good times as in bad times. We should never listen to the voice that tries to direct us away from the precepts taught in His word no matter how convincing the voice may sound.

All through our lives we will be faced with missed goals, crumbling dreams and at times we won't even know where we are in the grand scheme of things. But be assured Jesus is coming back. And when He does, He is going to be looking for a Church that is right where it is supposed to be.

Molly showed me that obeying the things that we have been taught are far more important than any sandcastles that we could ever build. On the very worst day of her little life, she still held fast to the things that she had been taught. How can we as children of the most high God do any less?

Chapter Twenty Two

RAPTURE FROM THE DEEP

"I was sinking deep in sin far from the peaceful shore: Very deeply stained within, sinking to rise no more: But the Master of the sea, heard my despairing cry. From the waters lifted me, now safe am I: Love lifted me......"

Recently while reading an article on rescue divers I was reminded of this old song. The training rescue personnel go through could well be applied to training we as Christians should undergo.

For divers most accidents happen while they are on top of the water. Similarly Christians are most often injured while they are still walking confidently with God. When exhaustion sets in, he finds himself a long way from shore or the safety of his vessel. He may be injured or tangled in nets, tossed and beaten from turbulent waves, burnt by the sun or pulled by strong currents. These dangers both spiritually and physically that we should help each other watch for. Prevention is much easier than reviving the injured.

There is a depth the scuba diver should never exceed, for when they do their blood becomes polluted due to the high pressure of the water surrounding them. A condition called nitrogen narcosis sets in. The narcotic effect of the nitrogen in their blood stream hinders the diver's ability to reason or respond quickly. Often they drown due to the fact the person no longer believes they need

their equipment. A person will discard their facemask and breathing apparatus to free themselves of the confines of their cumbersome equipment. This dazed condition is often call "Rapture of the Deep." There is also a depth that Christians can descend to where staying away from active prayer life and fasting lets the pressures of life began to pollute their heart.

soon they reach the point where they no longer believe that they need the Church, the Pastor, and finally God. In this confused condition they often leave the church and try to make it on their own, seeking freedom from any type of standards or restraints on their life. The result of this action is seen far to often. "....And when sin is finished it brings forth death".(James-1:15)

Before you can rescue someone, you must *recognize that the person is in trouble.* First access the situation. Helping an exhausted yourself afloat. It's up to you to know when to get the injured to more advanced help. You cannot know everything that's why we have Pastors, Teachers, Evangelist, Apostles, and Prophets. Every situation is different, the goal is the same but the treatment is different.

Slow down, it's their emergency not yours. Protect yourself, this is not selfish, it's good reasoning. The rescuer cannot help the situation if he is injured in the process. Stop, breathe, think and then act. Any rescuer could become the victim if he tries to make his own rules. You should be the only one to service your equipment, check it prior to each dive. You know what your own spiritual walk is like. Stay in shape. Learn to anticipate the consequences. If you are struggling, stop whatever activity you are engaged in. **Stress is always the result of circumstances, which cannot be changed!** If you can change the situation, stress will vanish. If you cannot change it, worry won't help. If thinking patterns are becoming a handicap, argue with yourself. When you believe that you don't know what to do, and that you're going to drown, you will. When it seems that the water is to cloudy, and you can't locate the group; maybe you're getting nervous.

Take control of the situation, slow down. Gain control of yourself before you go further. To blindly forge ahead just to keep moving could lead you away from safety. It's up to you to rise above your circumstance. From a higher vantage, you can always see where the others are at from the impact they are having on the surrounding environment. Then you can determine how to best rejoin them.

If we would pay attention to these tested life saving techniques. No matter what comes our way, we as well as countless others could be "Raptured from the deep".

Chapter Twenty Three

"PLEASE PRAY FOR ME!"
Came rushing in again, another hectic day,
Turned on my answering machine, and listened to it play.
My thoughts were interrupted, hearing a heartfelt plea,
A voice softly said, **"Please say a prayer for me."**
Then when thumbing through the mail, bills were all I could find,
until I saw a card near the bottom, with just a scribbled line.
A message so important, it was written there with care,
It caught my full attention, **"For me please say a prayer."**
Later I took a moment to read the paper, bad news came from everywhere,
then I read a small ad in the personals, Searching for someone to care,
It was shining like a beacon, easing my despair,
A plea written from the heart, **"Just say a little prayer."**
At a restaurant with some friends, we were relaxing for a while,
We extended kindness to the waitress, seeing tears behind her smile.
Picking up my check while exiting my chair, I
Noticed written across the bottom, **"Please remember me in prayer."**
At Church on Sunday evening, as the service began to end,
A man came down to the altar, looking for a friend.
Reaching towards the heavens, for all the world to see,
With tears the man was crying, **"Please say a prayer for me."**
Even waiting at the bus stop, while standing there in line,
I was reading the graffiti, to pass away the time.
Written there in paint, upon the dingy wall,
was a simple statement, **"Prayer can fix it all."**
Everywhere I'm turning, the cry keeps coming through,
The only thing I have going Lord, Is the fact that I know You.
Please listen to my heart Lord, sometime words are hard to say,
Because there are those who trust and depend on me, **"Please hear me when I pray!"**

Chapter Twenty Four

THE TEN CAMEL BRIDE

Several years ago, Readers Digest printed an article called "The Ten Camel Wife." In a third world country where the local custom was that a groom had to purchase his bride from her father, there emerged a story of considerable note. In a small village, where one goat or a couple of pigs would purchase a maiden of extraordinary beauty, a young man had broken all the village standards. He completely upset the balance of the local economy when he presented to his perspective father-in-law ten camels for the price of his bride.

The writer who reported this story soon sought out the young man to meet with him in hopes of finding out the reason that this bride cost so much. Surely, she must be the most beautiful lady in the whole country or maybe she was to become wealthy when she received her inheritance. There had to be some valid reason for this remarkable dowry. After meeting both the bride and the groom, the reporter began to interview the young man:

Reporter: *"I do not mean to be rude or unkind, but although your wife seems to be nice, I really expected her to very beautiful. Considering the fact that you gave ten camels for her, may I ask, why did you pay so much for her?"*

Groom: *"I suppose to some, she does look rather plain, but that is o.k., because she is the right bride for me, not others. I could easily have bought her for the price of one small sheep. But she was to be my wife for life and by purchasing her for ten camels, I set a value on her and this gave her a tremendous sense of self- worth. To begin with, no one else would have ever paid that kind of price for her, so I know she will always be faithful to me. She will be the mother of my children and no one will ever look down on my children, because I have made her royalty with my purchase and my children now come from a royal bloodline. Also, by giving this price for my bride, I have told the whole world how much I love her and how serious that I intend to fulfill my promises as her husband."*

A few days ago I was reminded of this story and I begin to think about the love of Christ. In a time when the sacrifice of a few sheep would insure that our sins would be rolled ahead for yet another year, the bridegroom Jesus stepped onto the scene and said, "I'll give my life for my bride the Church." The church may not be beautiful to others, but it is only intended to be His bride and because of the price that was paid, we are a royal bloodline. We are given the assurance that He will soon come to collect His blood-bought bride. As members of the "Bride of Christ" we should rejoice in the fact that He loved us enough to give His life. That alone gives us a value that no one could ever pay a higher price to obtain. Jesus said "I love this much," then He opened up His arms and they nailed him to a cross. No greater love has ever been shown since that day.

O.S. Davis penned a song that says: *The love of Jesus to me is greater, than anything else I've ever known, It reaches deeper, than any sinstain, It reaches higher than heaven's throne.* Oh, what a love. . . the love of Jesus!

Chapter Twenty Five

PECULIAR PEOPLE

"You got to see this," the cashier said excitedly. "Just as soon as Tammy gets here she is going to show it to us again."

There is a running joke between my brother-in -law and myself about the things I happen to encounter. He calls me a 'Nut-Magnet' because I seem to run into these situations more than anyone else does that he knows. Every time I visit him it is the same, sometime before I leave he will say, " I don't understand it, I live here and never run into these things until you come around." It may just be that I travel at a different pace than most other folks and the fact that I really do like people. Each one is so different and unique that I can't help wanting to observe for a while.

"Just wait and see it, your really going to like this," a tall guy put in. Turning to see who had spoken my gaze fell upon an elderly man. Tall, white hair and beard wearing a flat crown straw cowboy hat, tattered 'T-shirt and baggy overalls. With a toothless grin he spoke again. You ain't seen nothing like this, my Katy she's special I tell you."

Tammy soon arrived on the scene and we all gathered around in eager anticipation. Then with all the pride of a 4H-club member that just won first prize for the best hog at the county fair Katy pulled her hand from her pocket. Someone squealed in suprise (I hope it wasn't me) as we looked in amazement a Katy's right hand. There were six fingers on that hand. Soon she began demonstrating the mobility and abilities of having a second thumb. She could pick up things, pinch and scratch. Not being able to contain myself I had to ask her if it made picking bluegrass music on the guitar any easier or maybe playing the piano simpler. There have been times I would have given anything to have a couple of extra fingers (but that's another story). With a look of regret in her eyes she shook her head and said, no, it's not good for anything. It's just a another thumb." With that I turned and walked back to our table to join our party.

I watched as people from all over the little truck stop café, took their turn to come and look in amazement, make their comments and walk away shaking their heads. Finally when no one else came to look I saw a look of sadness cross her face and she turned to leave the building. Her fifteen minutes of fame was over. The whole situation grieved my heart.

What is it about peculiar a person that makes everyone want to look? Are we trying to reach a place where we feel better about ourselves because we are not the way that they are? I am not sure. I have noticed however that there are three types of people, peculiar people, people who cling to peculiar people and people who watch peculiar people (this in its self a bit odd). To be peculiar would imply that someone or something is different from the ordinary, not a standard or predictable occurrence. In the book of Romans, it says that we are to be a peculiar people, a royal priesthood an Holy nation. This means that the church is to be different from the ordinary, not tied to ritual or routine not focusing more on the program than the moving of the Spirit. We should stand out as light in our community. An encouragement to others examples and leaders in fields of labor. It does not mean that we should stand out as freaks in a side show in some rundown carnival.

For the church to be peculiar is a good thing, a status to be desired and we should endeavor to do our best to separate ourselves from blending into the background where we have nothing different to offer those who are bruised and hurting than they already are receiving.

There will always be those who hang around the church because it is different. They wont become Christians but enjoy being with them because where the real church is there is always excitement. They want to be known as being associated with it but wont commit their lives for fear that the price is too high or either they will fall into criticism form their peers. Still it is fun to be around the church.

Then there is a group that wants to come to see the show. They pass by every now and then to make sure the show is still in town, be entertained for a season and then walk away shaking their heads until another fire breaks out somewhere.

The later groups of people don't really bother me. They are receiving their rewards. It is the peculiar people I am concerned about. I mean what good is having six fingers if they can't do anything. If they exist as only ornaments and have no functional value they are of no use. If we are to become a peculiar people, a

This experience had such an impact on my friend, that anytime I would ever mention that restaurant or that particular dish he would refuse to discuss it further. And in all honesty I don't blame him. It is still my favorite meal, but the damage is done and I will have to find someone else to share it with.

The greatest experience I have ever had was when I made the conscious decision to allow Christ to reign in my life. From that day forward everything has been different. Life has been so good it is hard to explain. Naturally, I want to share this experience with everyone that I meet. I often wonder about my presentation. Do I present Christ to others properly, clear, and meaningful. Or do I just pour Him out all mixed up... Some formats are not the proper place to launch into a lengthy theological exposition. At those times, we must just let others see Him shining through us. And then there are the times that we do not act as Christians are supposed to act. Yet we try to witness to others, while we ourselves are misrepresenting Him. Often we mix our own inadequacies and failures with a blend of our testimonies and actions and then try to convince someone that they need what we have. Yet what we have is repulsive to others.

In Leviticus the Bible tells us not to have in our bag, diverse weights…And that we are to deal justly with everyone. We have to live it one way or the other. Jesus said that a spring couldn't bring forth both sweet and bitter water at the same time. A tree cannot bear two types of fruit and we cannot be Christians and willfully engage in sinful practices and then expect others to be impressed by our spirituality. As we approach each new person, we should ask ourselves, "How may I serve you?

Chapter Twenty Seven
Christmas Gift

I was into my fifth week of working ten to twelve hours a day and most weekends. The Christmas season had already hit our community and it seemed a drawback instead of an occasion of splendor, Christmas seemed to be represented only in the commercial aspects with crowded stores, bright lights. The smell of evergreens and everyone in a hurry. After all, Christmas for many is just a reference point that we tie the events of our life to. "You know that was just before Christmas," or "that happened just after Christmas," or "that happened right after Christmas vacation."

As a child, I would receive big, brightly colored packages, all neatly wrapped, which never exceeded or even fulfilled the preceding anticipation. There were many times that I spent Christmas day more than a little disappointed. Feeling like I should have gotten just one more gift. The presents I just knew that he was getting, somehow simply weren't there.

For me it had always made it easier for to understand why the Israelites didn't accept Jesus as the Messiah. They had it all planned out. The great Jehovah God would appear to the most elite of his priest and have all the answers to all of their hopes and dreams. Life would be marvelous, their trials would end and a New World order would begin. The first Christmas, like now was filled with excitement, that special feeling was in the air. The Messiah was soon to arrive. That first Christmas like so many of mine was a disaster - no King, no royal parade, no trumpets sounding and no great fanfare. As Christmas day began to unwrap, the only gift in the package was a baby. A small weak helpless baby. And not even royalty at that. He didn't seem like much of a gift to anyone but Mary and Joseph.

I remember finding myself standing in the emergency room of a nearby hospital scared and alone. I was watching the person that I loved the most in the world withering in with chest pains. Not being able to breathe. Suddenly the realization had hit me that I could lose Kay. Doctors, nurses and specialist running hurriedly about were saying, possible heart attack, hepatitis, liver disease and then not knowing. These things were repeated over and over in his mind. As I held her he began to call on Jesus my friend. Not a little baby, not a carpenter's son. Not the provider who fed the thousands with the loaves and fishes. Not the man who died on the cross. But the Great Physician, the mighty God, the Prince of Peace. Not knowing then what his answer would be, I called out. Then like now I began to reminisce of Christmases together with Kay. Not the negatives but the best times of his life as a married man. The first year I knew Jesus as my redeemer. We had played Mary and Joseph in the Christmas production. Then there was the year Kay scrimped and saved to buy me a new deer rifle. The one that I thought I couldn't live without. We had drove for hours to be with family with it hid under the car seat without me knowing that it was there. Just so that she could surprise me. I also remembered being away from home one Christmas on a business trip. The local pastor and his family and the church friends surrounding us and making us feel like part of their families. As we celebrated the season. Then there was the Christmas we bought each other a puppy that promptly ate a whole in the middle of the living room carpet. And we laughed together instead of crying. That day while I was remembering all of the good things in his life. I was reminded that during all of the good times and the bad. For me Jesus had always been there. A king would not have been approachable. A President surrounded by all of his aids would have been unattainable. But as if He were just waiting for me to mention his name, Jesus...the Messiah. The one I knew as a friend came walking into the hospital room. The greatest Christmas present that I had ever known gave Kay back to me.

Chapter Twenty Eight

TREES

I carefully inspected the holly branch I was holding in my left hand. It sure looked familiar to me but I could not remember where I had seen it before. Suddenly I knew where it came from, it was the limb that was supposed to be holding me up in this tree….On my decent the thought crossed my mind, "I must be allergic to trees."

You see all my life I have had this problem with trees, it seems that everywhere I go, (yes you guessed it) there is a tree. They come in every shape and size one could imagine. I'm beginning to think that they are following me, trying to find yet another clever way to injure or embarrass me. Yet I can't understand why. When I was just a lad several large trees tossed me on the ground from great heights simply because I was trying to pound boards into their limbs in order to build a tree house (how rude),

Then every year when the weather got cold I would have to help dad cut firewood and no matter where I stood, the tree would fall toward me. Barely escaping with my life I would survive each encounter sporting a large number of cuts and scratches. I'll have to admit that in the early days I didn't realize that they were after me (sometime I am slow to catch on to things) but as I get older it becomes more clear each year. At times I would be deer hunting and just as I was about to shoot, for no reason at all the tree in which I had my deer stand would begin to shudder and tremble, almost always causing me to miss a perfect shot on a record deer. And once without warning a tree tossed the whole deer stand and me out together, (a blatant disregard of my personal property if you ask me).

Three years ago at Christmas………….I answered a knock on the door of our home to find a stranger standing there. An older gentleman with a strange and fearful look on his face, His feet already poised in the 'ready to run' position carefully stated. " I hate to bother you, I'm your neighbor from across the street. And my old lady is not going to let me rest until I find out what is going on over here." Not understanding what he meant I urged him to continue hoping myself to find out what was going on over here. "Well you

see you have got that large picture window over there." "Yes"
"Well the curtain is open and from our house we can see right inside
this room ." That made me more than a little uncomfortable. "And
that's what has my wife so upset, first it's there and then it's not.
Then it's over there, and now it's back, then it completely disappears
and reappears. Are you doing some kind of black magic over here?
This just isn't right."

Three weeks before Christmas Kay and I sat down to try to
decide what we would buy each other for a Christmas gift. Having
run out of space for the toys we already had acquired we decided
that we would do something for the house instead. New Carpet, that
would be our mutual gift to each other. On the way home from the
carpet center Kay made mention that she really didn't like the color
of the study. It just wouldn't look right with the new carpet we
picked out And If I was going to repaint it had to be in the next
couple of days before the new carpet arrived. Carpet installers will
move furniture (not Christmas trees). Our tree (a big one) was
already up, lit, decorated, tinseled and stared. No one is brave
enough to decorate the same tree twice in the same year so I came
up with a plan. Retrieving a furniture dolly from the garage I lay on
the floor while Kay steadied the tree and we wrestled it up upon the
dolly. (The tree took this opportunity to fill the back of my shirt with
stickers and add a scratch or two for vengeance to my face). Nothing
is more depressing than a Christmas tree that is not lit up so we drug
out an extension cord to power the thing up. Now we had mobility,
As I painted and moved furniture around I could just push the tree
ahead of me out of my way. I never dreamed it would upset the
neighbors like that.

Walking away shaking his head all he could say was, "too
weird, that's just too weird." I saw a moving truck in front of their
house a few weeks later. Oh, well score another one for the trees,
now all my neighbors watch me suspiciously. Have you ever notice
how gentle and lovely a tree is when the sun is out and shining
brightly. But I tell you there is something sinister about a tree. If you
have ever been alone deep in the woods when darkness fell you will
testify that what I am about to say is true. As soon as the light goes
out the tree takes on menacing shapes like that of monsters. Twisted
and ugly, whispering to each other. Reaching for you and tearing at

Chapter Thirty

CHOICE

I sat at his desk working late updating reports for the quarterly statements that were due. The young lady quietly hummed to herself as she dusted the furniture and emptied the trash containers in his office. Breaking the silence Ben looked up from his work and asked.

"Well Miss Hope, we have a long weekend coming up in a couple of days. Do you have any big plans this weekend?"

"No, not really," Diane answered. "I guess that I am just going to hang around some. Tonight I thought I would get my nails done. Tomorrow I am going to hang out at the mall and then catch the evening matinee at the cinema. Then Saturday I am going to have an abortion. Sunday some friends are coming over and...."

I dropped my pen in surprise. I didn't hear a word after she said abortion. Abortion, I had never known anyone that had even considered abortion. As far as I knew, much less anyone that had actually planned to have one. And to be able to talk about it as casually as getting her nails done. Instantly I felt like throwing up. I felt both burning hot and freezing cold at the same time. Something like you feel when you witness a car accident from a distance and helplessly you watch unable to stop it from happening. An oppressing feeling filled the room. Fighting the tears from my eyes, I gasp. Clearing my throat I spoke. "You're kidding right?"

"No, I'm really going to have an abortion."

"You mean you're pregnant? I mean I didn't know that you were married. You never mentioned your husband before."

"No, I'm not married, you don't have to be married to get pregnant you know."

"Of course I knew that," I stammered. "I mean I just didn't know...Who is the fa... Oh I'm sorry. I mean I know that it is none of my business. I didn't mean to intrude."

"It's OK," Diane said. "I knew what I was getting into when I did it. It's bound to happen sooner or later. It's just the price you have to pay. It could happen to anyone, it just happened to me this time that's all. But I'll get it taken care of this weekend and then it will all be over. I should have known better than to fool around with a married man anyway."

"Married," I gasped. I couldn't believe the things that I was hearing. "Married, does he know that you're going to do this?"

"Naw, I didn't even bother to tell him, it wouldn't matter anyway. He has too much going on to get tied up in the kind of problems that this would cause. He doesn't even know that I am pregnant. Besides if I had the baby I would have to quit my job. Then who would pay the bills? I barely make it now on what I earn. I couldn't even pay the doctor bills let alone miss work and then there would be childcare. Forget it, I'm not ready for any of that yet. I have my whole life in front of me. Besides it's my right to decide what goes on inside my body. The Supreme Court say's it's Ok so I don't see anything wrong with it." The frustration shown clearly on her face as tears began to cloud her eyes.

Hurrying to gather her things together Diane Hope turned to leave the room. Clearly she did not intend to continue the conversation any further. Ben felt as if he had to do something, only he had no idea what to do. Almost shouting while trying to detain her I cried, "Wait, please wait for just a second."

Looking back at me over her shoulder she said, "Yes."

"Would you let me take you to lunch tomorrow?"

"What for?" Diane looked at me with eyes full of suspicion.

"Well, I thought I would try to talk you out of having the abortion."

"It's no use, I told you. I have already thought it all out."

"Please!"

"You gonna pay for the meal?"

"Sure."

"Well I guess I can't turn down a free meal, now can I. Alright I'll go with you. But I'm warning you it won't do any good." With that she left the room.

I sat there staring at the closed door. "Oh, Lord," I said. "What is going to happen next? What am I supposed to tell her? I don't know anything about this subject. I don't even know how to find out what to say."

I stopped his work for the day and started home in the gathering dusk. Fighting the crowd walking along the busy sidewalk

I pushed his way along lost in thought. After walking several blocks I realized that I had passed the entrance to the subway station that he usually used. Turning to go back in the direction from which I had come. I realized that the press of the crowd would not allow me to return in the direction from which I had come. Ahead down the sidewalk about two blocks I could see the red and green sign that marked another subway entrance. Figuring it would be easier to continue on instead of turning back I started walking. Upon reaching the subway entrance I turned to enter the stairwell when across the street to my surprise I saw a sign hanging above a small storefront. The sign read 'Pro-Life Center, Abortion is Murder, You Have A Choice'. I stood frozen to the spot where I was standing.

"Come on, move it buddy. You're blocking the stairs. Get out of the way. We ain't got all day." Like a moth drawn to a flame I did not realize what I was doing as he began to move across the street to the entrance of the small anti-abortion center. Standing in the entrance to the door, I closed his eyes and prayed. " Lord let me find the wisdom I need to keep Diane from killing her baby." With that I pushed the door open and entered as a small bell rang somewhere in the back of the building.

I sat across the table from Diane Hope at the tiny Italian restaurant down the street from where we worked. I was so nervous that I could hardly decide what to order. The waiter brought the salads and both me and Diane ate in silence for a few moments. I could not make my eyes meet those of my young friend. So much was riding on the outcome of this meeting, and I didn't even know where to begin.

Finally Diane broke the silence. "I thought you brought me to lunch to talk me out of it." she said.

"I did," I answered.

"So start talking already. We haven't got all day. And this is the only chance that your going to get," her voice filled with sarcasm.

"Well, ah, to be quiet honest with you I really didn't know much about the subject. That is except for what the bible says about it. So I spent the greatest part of last evening with the people down at the pro-life center finding out all about abortion. You see in my heart I knew that it was wrong but it wasn't until I found out what they really do that I realized how horrible it is."

"Wait a minute; did you say the bible said it was wrong? Let's just take it one step at a time. What did the bible say?"

"Ok, you know one of the commandments says *Thou shall not kill* right. Well I found a place where Solomon said. You do know who Solomon was don't you. He was the wisest man that ever lived. Well Solomon said *From the moment of conception a soul is breathed into a child* or something to that affect. But what I found out last night is horrible. You see when they do an abortion the first thing that they have to do is to kill the baby."

"It's not a baby yet, it's just an egg."

"No, you're wrong it is a baby. It has arms and legs. It moves it feels things. Any way what they do is they have to reach up inside of you and cut the baby into small enough pieces to remove them from your body through your natural openings you understand. Then they take a vacuum machine and suck out all of the parts. And if the head is too large to come out they have to reach in and crush it, kind of like you would crush a pecan. Then they suck that out too. When they get all of the parts out. They have to reassemble the whole baby. To make sure that they didn't leave any parts inside. That would cause infection. They tell me that for the rest of your life every time you hear a vacuum cleaner motor running, you feel sick all over again. I know that they told you that it wouldn't hurt. But it will, you will be sick for several days possibly with lots of bleeding. But let me tell you what else I found out. These abortion clinics don't perform abortions just because they are nice. Or because they want to protect your rights to do what you want with your body. They make a lot of money doing the abortions. Not only do they make money from people like you who pay them to do it. But they also sell the fetus. Yes your baby is a *'cash crop'*. They sell the fetus to major cosmetic companies to make women's makeup."

"What!"

"Yes they sell the fetus. The cosmetic companies takes it and cooks it, then it is ground into a powder and mixed with other chemicals that make women's makeup. If you're wearing makeup right now you might be wearing someone's baby on your face. What do think about that."

Diane's eyes begin to fill with tears.

"Not only are they doing that, but now they have a law that say's that they can abort a baby as long as any of the baby's body is still in the mother. So when your baby is being born they can kill it just as long as a hand or foot or something is still inside. I call that murder don't you."

Diane was speechless. Tears were now flowing freely down both of their faces.

I said, "Now I want to show you something." I handed her a card on which was listed all the statistics about a six week old baby. How he is formed. How he moves. What he feels and so forth. As Diane began to read the card she began shaking her head from side to side saying quietly to her self, "No, no, no."

It read: *Everyone's Biography - Heartbeat begins between the eighteenth and twenty fifth days. Foundation for the entire nervous system is laid down by the twentieth day. At forty-two days the skeleton is complete, reflexes are present. Electrical brain waves have been recorded as early as forty-three days. The brain and all body systems are present by eight weeks. At eight weeks if we tickle the baby's nose he will flex his head backward away from the stimulus. At nine to ten weeks he squints, swallows, moves his tongue, and if you stroke his palm he will make a fist. At eleven to twelve weeks he sucks his thumb vigorously and breathes his amniotic fluid to develop the organs of respiration. Fingernails are present by eleven to twelve weeks, eyelashes by sixteen. All body systems are functioning by twelve weeks.*

I reached across the table and took her hand. In my hand I held a life-size doll. A replica of a six week old fetus. Approximately two and one half inches long. Curled in a fetal position you could plainly see hands, arms, feet legs, mouth, nose, eyelids and ears. It was clear that this was a baby. Dropping the doll into Diane outstretched hand Be I said. "This is what your baby looks like today."

"No, they told me it was just an egg. An egg you know like a chicken egg or something. Not like this, this is a baby. I'm not gonna let any body kill my baby. They lied to me. Nobody is going to sell my baby to make money. Why don't somebody tell the people what their doing. This just isn't right. How can they do this? Well I tell you what they are not going to hurt my baby, not as long as I can do something about it. I am going to have this baby."

People in the restaurant looked on in wonder as Diane and I embraced. Tears running unchecked down both of our faces we sobbed and held each other.

"Thank you, thank you," she said. "Thank you for caring Greg Bullock.

As we left the restaurant I knew that I would never in my life forget the meal that they didn't eat.